Published by

James H. Kaster

Concord, NC

Printed in the United States of America

ISBN: 978-0-982-82209-8

The information contained within this book is true and complete to the best of my knowledge. Material was gathered from manufacturers' brochures, advertisements and media kits. Information is provided without any guarantee on the part of the publisher. Publisher also disclaims any liability incurred from use of this information.

© 2011 by James H. Kaster

All rights reserved. No part of this publication may be reproduced or transmitted in any form or by any means, electronic or mechanical, including photocopy, scanning, recording or any information retrieval system without permission in writing from the publisher. Permission is never granted for commercial purposes.

Manufacturer, vehicle, model, trim names and/or designations are the trademarks of their respective companies. They are used for identification purposes only. This is not an official publication of any of these companies or manufacturers.

Table of Contents

Table of Contents	2
The Personal Luxury Car	3
Buick	4
Cadillac	16
Chevrolet	25
Chrysler	30
Continental	36
Dodge	37
Ford	41
Imperial	53
Lincoln	54
Mercury	63
Oldsmobile	70
Pontiac	77
Studebaker	83
Specifications	86
Honorable Mention	88
Index	92

1966 Pontiac Grand Prix
"So beautiful, in fact, its clean, aristocratic lines have set the standard for personal luxury cars."

1966 Ford Thunderbird
"America's personal luxury car."

Personal Luxury Cars

As the car market multiplied with many styles, makes and functions, one particular trend elevated the automobile above the mere transportation-only, family-hauling and/or workhorse appliance. It was the "Personal Luxury Car." Affordable cars could be crafted and massaged into status symbols for the masses while luxury cars could be similarly fashioned into a rarer form of distinction. This new found prominence, supposedly, mitigated the chores of daily driving and errand running through environmental isolation; all the while projecting the owner's individuality and ego to the world.

The very definition of a Personal Luxury Car varies from person to person as its meaning differs based on one's experiences or desires from such a car. Because the definition varies, so do the automobiles that may be classified as such. For this book, then, I had to open my mind to the possibilities, find some common grounds and identify the characteristics. I started with some basic associations of the words.

"Personal"
- Sense of uniqueness, distinction or individuality
- It's about image and confidence
- Designed for the driver first, passengers second; subsequently, it is not a typical family hauler

"Luxury"
- Material and appointment choices above the offerings of the mainstream models
- Aura of scarcity and rarity that is not intended to be the make's volume sales leader
- Restricted body, styling and model name combination – though some aspects of any of these might be shared with the make's other models, the overall amalgamation should be dissimilar. It should be a single body line; two-door only or four-door only. Proliferation of body styles with a single model name creates mass-appeal which is opposed to the luxury concept of exclusivity.
- Tuned for touring power and comfort over street pounding performance

Marketing managers seized the growing opportunity for buyers' need of self expression and filled promotional materials with glowing adjectives to describe the attributes of these cars. These vivid words can be found in most dealer literature: *appointed, character, comfortable, commanding, discriminating, distinctive, elegant, exclusive, fashionable, formidable, glamorous, individualistic, international, lavish, poised, tasteful, unique* and more.

From these definitions, one model, more than any other epitomizes the "Personal Luxury Car" for five decades: the Ford Thunderbird. In fact, in its first model year of 1955, Ford markets the Thunderbird, in the brochure, as "A personal car of distinction…"

But, is the Thunderbird the first Personal Luxury Car? That is debatable. In 1955, Chrysler released the C-300. While promoted as a performance car, it had good touring manners as well. Chrysler would use the words "distinctive" and "discriminating" to describe the C-300. And before these two cars, starting in 1953, Studebaker had the Commanders, Champions and Presidents whose higher trim level coupes embodied the traits of the Personal Luxury Car. But, by sharing the same name as the four-door and wagon models, the cachet of personal luxury was diluted. Studebaker remedied this by originating a new name for these coupes in 1956 through 1964 as the Hawk series. Not to be excluded, vehicles such as the fore-mentioned Studebakers, and others like the Cutlass Supreme and more, are described in the Honorable Mentions section of the book.

For many, "Personal Luxury Car" is synonymous with "Personal Luxury Coupe". Yet, I believe there are examples of four-door sedans that push the envelope of the personal luxury definition. These cars exhibit the same characteristics of "personal" and "luxury" while offering smaller dimensions than the make's typical full-size cars. Examples include the Cadillac Seville, Lincoln Versailles and Lincoln Continental.

Additionally, Personal Luxury Cars could be 2-seaters that were built to be touring cars, not sports cars. The original Thunderbird, Cadillac Allanté, Buick Reatta and Chrysler's TC by Maserati all fit into this category. Perhaps this is better called the Personal Luxury Roadster.

By the mid- to late 1980s, the Personal Luxury Car begins the transformation to sports coupes and sports sedans with a greater emphasis on handling dynamics over driving comfort and isolation associated with luxury. This new luxury becomes performance-oriented with the full complement of appointments and power assists.

In this book, two stars are denoted to indicate two series of the Personal Luxury Car.

 The Silver Star is used on Upscale models. Upscale models are generally based on a manufacturer's family sedan with affordability being the key value for entry into a Personal Luxury Car.

 The Gold Star is reserved for Premium models which represent a prestige level, high-priced automobile with exclusivity as one of its key values.

Also included, quotes from media kits, brochures and advertising provide an insight into how the manufacturers were selling a lifestyle.

- James H. Kaster

Buick Reatta 1988-1991

1988 Buick Reatta

1989 Buick Reatta dash panel

1990 Buick Reatta dash panel

1991 Buick Reatta

1991 Buick Reatta convertible

1989: "The Reatta driver has tabled some of life's personal gratifications on the way to achieving a secure position in life. Reatta is an ideal award for all those long hours and hard work."

1989: "As Buick's premium American 2-seater, Reatta embodies the idea that luxury and comfort are not incompatible with sportiness and roadworthiness."

1988 Buick Reatta interior

American Automotive Design Trends: The Personal Luxury Car

Buick Regal 1978-1980

1979: "Buick Regal. Luxurious. Roomy. Sophisticated. It's a personal, mid-size car designed with you in mind."

1979 Buick Regal Limited Coupe

Starting in 1973, Regal began as a trim level on the Century family car platform. In 1978, Regal becomes a unique, upscale model as a 2-door only coupe.

1980 Buick Regal Sport Coupe

1978 Buick Regal Sport Coupe

1978: "In short, what we've done with the 1978 Regal is lavish it with science to make it fun to drive. And we've touched it with magic, too, to preserve the luxury and comfort you've come to expect of the Buick name."

1980 Regal Limited interior

1980: "The mid-size personal luxury car. The genre seems to have captivated America the way convertibles and two door hardtops once did. This year there are not three, but four distinct Regals to choose from. The Regal Coupe, the prestigious uptown Regal Limited, the turbocharged Regal Sport Coupe and a new, Limited Edition, Regal Somerset."

1980 Regal Somerset Limited Edition interior

Regal dash panel

1980 Regal Somerset Limited Edition Coupe

American Automotive Design Trends: The Personal Luxury Car

Buick Regal 1981, 1985-1987

1985 Buick Regal Limited

From 1982 – 1984, Regal is offered as both a two- and four-door model. As a multi-line model, their luxury appeal is diminished.

1981 Buick Regal Limited

1981 Buick Regal Coupe

<u>1981</u>: "The Regal and Regal Limited are personal luxury cars with a time-honoured sense of luxury about them. The Regal T Type, however, gives that emphasis a decided shift toward high performance."

1981 Buick Regal Dash Panel

Buick, like most manufacturers of the time, began a new marketing and technological migration strategy in the mid-eighties. While there was still a demand for personal luxury cars, there was also a growing market for the return of muscle cars. And manufacturers responded by creating more powerful and more responsive rides like this 1985 Buick Regal Grand National, below.

1985 Buick Regal Dash Panel

1985 Buick Regal Grand National

Buick Regal 1988-1989

1988 Buick Regal

In 1990, Buick re-introduces a four-door model to the line-up, again diminishing the exclusivity factor expected by Personal Luxury Car buyers.

1988 Buick Regal

1988: "The distinctively sculpted 1988 Regal's shape combines efficiency and beauty. The end result is the lowest coefficient of drag of any Buick ever."

"There's nothing else like it on the American road. The values held by the Regal owner are clearly reflected in the characteristics of the new Regal: quality, excellence of design and execution and – above all – that special spirited beauty that belongs only to automobiles that bear the Buick hallmark."

1988 Buick Regal interior

1989 Buick Regal dash panel

1989: "Regal's instruments and controls are a further exhibition of its quite good taste."

American Automotive Design Trends: The Personal Luxury Car

Buick Riviera 1963-1965

1963 Buick Riviera

1963: "America's bid for a great new international classic car."

1963 Buick Riviera

1963 Buick Riviera

1963 Buick Riviera

1965 Buick Riviera

1963: "Actually, the feeling you're supposed to get from sitting in the driver's seat is that you are in command of a pretty formidable piece of machinery - which you are."

1965 Buick Riviera
    Buick introduces a Gran Sport option in 1965 with a 425CID V-8, high-performance 3.42 to 1 rear axle ratio, special wheel covers and more.

1965: "Think of a car that is loaded with action, classic in line, agile as a cat, and luxurious beyond belief."

American Automotive Design Trends: The Personal Luxury Car

Buick Riviera 1966-1970

1966: "...a totally tuned car"

1966 Buick Riviera

1966 Buick Riviera

1966 Buick Riviera dash panel

1968 Buick Riviera dash panel

1968 Buick Riviera

1966: "Inside...nothing less than the best."

1967: "An automobile whose styling, performance, ride and handling have been honed to a fine edge attained by few of the world's automobiles."

1966 Buick Riviera

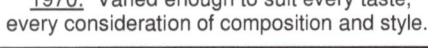

1970: "Varied enough to suit every taste, every consideration of composition and style."

1970 Buick Riviera

American Automotive Design Trends: The Personal Luxury Car

Buick Riviera 1971-1973

1973 Buick Riviera

1971 Buick Riviera

1973 Buick Riviera interior

1971 Buick Riviera dash panel

1971: "Riviera is elegance turned on."

1971 Buick Riviera

1971 Buick Riviera interior

1971 Buick Riviera door panel

American Automotive Design Trends: The Personal Luxury Car

Buick Riviera 1974-1976

1974 Buick Riviera

1974 Buick Riviera

1974 Buick Riviera interior

1976 Buick Riviera

1975 Buick Riviera

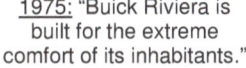
1975: "Buick Riviera is built for the extreme comfort of its inhabitants."

1976 Buick Riviera

1974 Buick Riviera dash panel

1976: "A road car; a luxury car. It's two of the nicest cars you've ever wanted."

American Automotive Design Trends: The Personal Luxury Car

Buick Riviera 1977-1978

![1978 Buick Riviera]

1978 Buick Riviera

1978 Buick Riviera interior & dash panel

1978: "The Riviera. It was originally conceived to be a leader in a personal luxury car design.

The 1978 Riviera enjoys a clean uncluttered look, from front to back. Opera windows distinguish its profile, while the 'spoked look' of its wheel covers embellish its classic car orientation.

On the road, front and rear stabilizer bars, plus hefty shocks, and computer-selected coil springs at each wheel help to ensure smooth going. Other standard driving assists include power steering. Power front disc brakes. Or, if you prefer, 4-wheel disc brakes.

Standard power in Riviera is provided by a 350 CID (5.7 litre) V-8 with 4-barrel carburetion. But for those who want more power, a 403 CID (6.6 litre) 4-barrel V-8 is available.

But there is another, and equally alluring, side to Riviera's nature. That of the elegantly appointed luxury coupe.

Plush, crushed-velour seats are arranged in 50/50 fashion to allow the driver to independently adjust his position at the wheel.

Standard features include twin armrests, power windows, instruments set in what looks like polished burled walnut, and thickly padded three-spoke steering wheel.

All this makes for something that is more than mere transportation. Because to drive the Riviera is to experience both the magic of Buick luxury and the science of communication with the road."

American Automotive Design Trends: The Personal Luxury Car

Buick Riviera 1979-1985

1979 Buick Riviera

1981 Buick Riviera T Type

1985 Buick Riviera Convertible

1985: "With an interior space that exudes a comfortable intimacy between driver and machine."

1981 Buick Riviera T TYPE interior

1981: "…it is the balance of design, the careful use of special materials, and creative execution that makes Riviera the success that it is."

1980 Buick Riviera interior

1981 Buick Riviera dash panel

1984: "Comfort abounds, providing luxury in exceptional amounts."

American Automotive Design Trends: The Personal Luxury Car

Buick Riviera 1986-1993

1986 Buick Riviera

1986: "This is a high-performance grand touring machine, yes. But, Riviera accomplishes that mission without sacrificing luxury or comfort. The appointments are exquisite, the ride smooth, silent, unobtrusive."

1986 Buick Riviera dash panel and interior

1986: "The interior of the Riviera is a study in tailored elegance. A sensory experience."

1989 Buick Riviera

1989: "...the person to whom Riviera appeals is also a breed set apart: style-conscious, an arbiter of good taste and sure of what he or she wants."

Disappointing sales of the 1986-1988 models resulted in a refresh of the platform that increased the overall length of the car in 1989.

1986 Buick Riviera T Type

1993 Buick Riviera

1993 Buick Riviera interior

1993: "Tailored to handle the road and you…"

1993 Buick Riviera dash panel

American Automotive Design Trends: The Personal Luxury Ca

Buick Riviera 1995-1999

1995 Buick Riviera

1995 Buick Riviera interior

1995 Buick Riviera dash panel

1995: "Everyone won. The stylists. The engineers. The sculptors. The safety devotees and the comfort team and the test track drivers. And, most of all, you. This is a car that speaks to the achiever in all of us; that part of us that quietly, intensely, urges us beyond the norm – to do something better than anyone else can do it."

1995 Buick Riviera

American Automotive Design Trends: The Personal Luxury Car

Cadillac Allanté 1987-1993

1987 Cadillac Allanté

1988 Cadillac Allanté dash panel

1987 Cadillac Allanté interior

1988: "For those who are fortunate enough to write their own rules…"

1988 Cadillac Allanté

1993 Cadillac Allanté

American Automotive Design Trends: The Personal Luxury Car

Cadillac Eldorado 1967-1970

1967: "World's finest personal car."

1967 Cadillac Eldorado

1967 Cadillac Eldorado interior

1967 Cadillac Eldorado

1967: "Eldorado... dramatic blend of the best of two motoring worlds. This brilliant new Cadillac combines the spirit and action of a true performance car with the comfort and five-passenger spaciousness of a true luxury car."

1970 Cadillac Eldorado interior

1970 Cadillac Eldorado

1970: "Purposely built to be the world's finest personal car, the Fleetwood Eldorado is that unique automotive creation: One designed for the motorist who desires unusual spirited performance, individual styling and all the elegance and comfort for which Cadillac is renowned."

American Automotive Design Trends: The Personal Luxury Car

Cadillac Eldorado 1971-1978

1971: "With its distinctive individuality, Eldorado is unquestionably the world's most elegant personal car."

1971 Cadillac Eldorado

1971: "Only Eldorado combines such tasteful individuality and youthful sportiness in one great personal car."

1971 Cadillac Eldorado Convertible

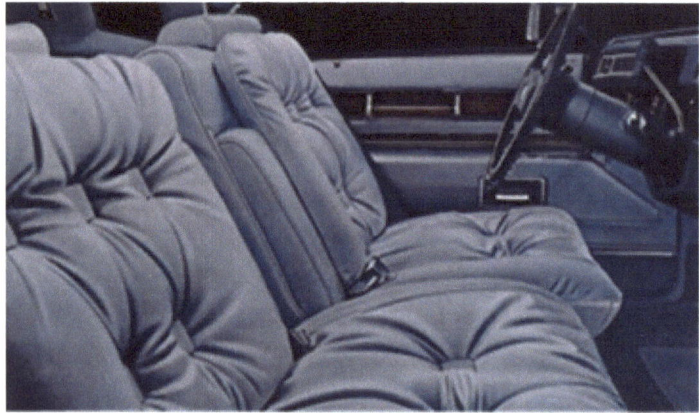

1978 Cadillac Eldorado Biarritz interior

1977 Cadillac Eldorado Biarritz

1974: "Luxury, comfort and convenience in a personal size car."

1972 Cadillac Eldorado interior

Cadillac Eldorado 1979-1985

1979: "The new breed of Eldorado. One of the world's best engineered cars."

1979 Cadillac Eldorado

1979 Cadillac Eldorado interior

1980 Cadillac Eldorado Biarritz

1984 Cadillac Eldorado Convertible

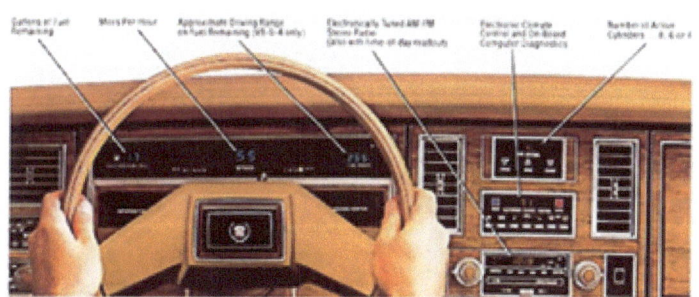

1981 Cadillac Eldorado dash panel

1983: "to combine the sportiness of a custom personal car with the comfort and engineering innovation of a great luxury car."

1983 Cadillac Eldorado Touring Coupe

American Automotive Design Trends: The Personal Luxury Car

Cadillac Eldorado 1986-1991

1986: "Above all, it's the feeling of uncompromising excellence."

1986 Cadillac Eldorado interior

1986 Cadillac Eldorado

1988: "The Eldorado Biarritz has been created for those discerning individuals who want even more luxury. Even more distinctive styling. Even more comfort."

1986 Cadillac Eldorado Biarritz

1988 Cadillac Eldorado Biarritz (Cadillac adds 3" in length in 1988)

1986 Cadillac Eldorado dash panel

Cadillac Eldorado 1992-2002

1997 Cadillac Eldorado dash panel

1997: "Eldorado's arresting style and spirit of freedom create the perfect statement for those who set their own pace."

1997 Cadillac Eldorado

American Automotive Design Trends: The Personal Luxury Car

Cadillac Seville 1975-1979

1976 Cadillac Seville

1976 Cadillac Seville rear seat interior

1976 Cadillac Seville interior

1978 Cadillac Seville Elegante

> 1975: "This is the first American car to combine international size, styling and performance with Cadillac comfort and convenience."
>
> 1976: "A new dimension in luxury car driving."
>
> 1978: "Understated; yet exquisitely appointed for your personal comfort and convenience."

1977 Cadillac Seville dash panel below

American Automotive Design Trends: The Personal Luxury Car

Cadillac Seville 1980-1985

1980 Cadillac Seville Elegante

1980 Cadillac Seville interior

> 1980: "Seville… quite possibly the most distinctive car in the world today… and the most advanced."

1983 Cadillac Seville optional digital instrumentation

1981 Cadillac Seville

1983 Cadillac Seville

1983 Cadillac Seville with Cabriolet roof option

Cadillac Seville 1986-1991

1987 Cadillac Seville Elegante

1987 Cadillac Seville Elegante interior

1987: "Seville. The elegant spirit of Cadillac"

1987 Cadillac Seville

1987 Cadillac Seville interior

American Automotive Design Trends: The Personal Luxury Car

Cadillac Seville 1992-1997

1997 Cadillac Seville

1997 Cadillac Seville interior

Cadillac Seville 1998-2004

1998 Cadillac Seville interior

1998: "Virtually nothing has been compromised. Except, perhaps, for the esteem of every other performance luxury sedan on the planet."

2004 Cadillac Seville

1998 Cadillac Seville

Chevrolet Monte Carlo 1970-1972

1970 Chevrolet Monte Carlo

1972 Chevrolet Monte Carlo

1970 Chevrolet Monte Carlo dash panel

1972: "America's most attainable luxury car."

1972 Chevrolet Monte Carlo

1970 Chevrolet Monte Carlo optional bucket seats

1970: "Monte Carlo is a side of Chevrolet you've never known before. The correct British would title it a 'gentleman's car.'"

1970: "Monte Carlo is a driver's car that only a handful of American-made cars have anything in common with."

American Automotive Design Trends: The Personal Luxury Car

Chevrolet Monte Carlo 1973-1977

1973 Chevrolet Monte Carlo S

1973: "Its qualities of elegance, quiet, comfort and the relaxing stability, result in a personal luxury car of the first rank: a car which combines American comfort with European handling."

1973 Chevrolet Monte Carlo dash panel

1975 Chevrolet Monte Carlo   1977 Chevrolet Monte Carlo

1974 Chevrolet Monte Carlo interior

1973 Chevrolet Monte Carlo optional swivel bucket seats

1974: "As elegant mechanically as it is in appearance."

1975: "…neat in size, agile and responsive - a superb driving experience."

1977: "…Monte Carlo was conceived as a highly individual, very personal automobile that would appeal to a particularly discriminating buyer."

Chevrolet Monte Carlo 1978-1980

1978: "You can see it in the stately stance and sculpted sides. You can feel it in the way a Monte Carlo moves. It is a car beautifully in tune with the times, yet emphatically apart from the crowd."

1978 Chevrolet Monte Carlo Sport Coupe

1978 Chevrolet Monte Carlo dash panel & bucket seats

1979 Chevrolet Monte Carlo interior options

1980 Chevrolet Monte Carlo

1979 Chevrolet Monte Carlo   1980 Chevrolet Monte Carlo

1979: "It's your own personal 'driver's suite.'"

American Automotive Design Trends: The Personal Luxury Car

Chevrolet Monte Carlo 1981-1988

1981 Chevrolet Monte Carlo Landau Coupe

1983 Chevrolet Monte Carlo

1981 Chevrolet Monte Carlo Sports Coupe

1984 Chevrolet Monte Carlo CL Custom interior

1981: "It is a personal car with an almost uncanny ability to turn heads."

1984: "Personal Style. Road car performance."

1985: "Classic elegance tailored to your taste."

1983 Chevrolet Monte Carlo dash panel

Chevrolet Monte Carlo 1995-1999

Chevrolet Monte Carlo 2000-2007 ★

2005 Chevrolet Monte Carlo LT

1999 Chevrolet Monte Carlo LS

2000 Chevrolet Monte Carlo

1999: "On the outside, its styling is a sophisticated indulgence in steel. On the inside, this is a driver's car, with four-wheel independent suspension, front-wheel-drive traction and a rigid body structure for a solid feel on the road."

2005 Chevrolet Monte Carlo Supercharged SS

American Automotive Design Trends: The Personal Luxury Car

Chrysler 300 Letter Series 1955-1956

1955: "Smartly, superbly different and distinctive."

1956 Chrysler 300B

1956 Chrysler 300B

1955: "- a car with a contemporary look of style and smartness - a car with the feel, the response, and the road hugging look of European sports cars - and one that would reflect the discriminating good taste of the owner."

1955: "…a platinum colored beauty of class and distinction…"

1955 Chrysler C-300

1955 Chrysler C-300

Chrysler 300 Letter Series 1957-1959

1957: "America's greatest performing car."

1957 Chrysler 300C

1957 Chrysler 300C

1957: "Depending on what you're looking for, the Chrysler 300-C is either a luxury motor car with the power and "feel" of a sports car… or it is the only sports car with the elegance and comfort of a limousine."

1957 Chrysler 300C

1958 Chrysler 300D

1959 Chrysler 300E

American Automotive Design Trends: The Personal Luxury Car

Chrysler 300 Letter Series 1960-1961

1961: "A rare kind of car for a rare kind of man."

1961 Chrysler 300G

In 1962, Chrysler introduces the 300 as a full line model with the letter series continuing the luxury/performance heritage.

Chrysler Cordoba 1975-1979

1978 Chrysler Cordoba

1975 Chrysler Cordoba

1975 Chrysler Cordoba

1975: "…the new small Chrysler"
1975: "It offers a highly personalized, planned environment."
1976: "By design, a personal automobile."

1977: "A personal automobile of marked distinction and character…"
1978: "Very personal. Very formal. The very picture of style."
1979: "The personal car with the luxury touch."

1976 Chrysler Cordoba

1977 Chrysler Cordoba

1978 Chrysler Cordoba

1979 Chrysler Cordoba

1975 Chrysler Cordoba
Standard velour interior / 1975 Chrysler Cordoba Optional leather bucket seats

1977 Chrysler Cordoba
Optional Checkmate cloth

1978 Chrysler Cordoba
Optional bucket seats

American Automotive Design Trends: The Personal Luxury Car

Chrysler Cordoba 1980-1983

1980 Chrysler Cordoba

1980 Chrysler Cordoba

1980: "...a car whose striking new, resized form strides into the new decade with poise and assurance befitting its proud tradition."

1982: "...the very sophisticated Chrysler."

1982 Chrysler Cordoba LS with optional bucket seats

1981 Chrysler Cordoba dash panel and interior

Chrysler's TC by Maserati 1989-1991

1989 Chrysler's TC by Maserati

1990 Chrysler's TC by Maserati

1990 Chrysler's TC by Maserati

1990 Chrysler's TC by Maserati

1990 Chrysler's TC by Maserati

American Automotive Design Trends: The Personal Luxury Car

Continental Mark II 1956-1957

1956: "The Continental Mark II is the work of master craftsmen."

1956 Continental Mark II

In 1958, the Continental becomes a full model line and in 1959 the division is eliminated and the Continental becomes a Lincoln model.

1956 Continental Mark II

1956 Continental Mark II

1957 Continental Mark II

1957 Continental Mark II

Dodge Charge SE 1975-1978

1977: "Quiet, sleek, luxurious - Charger SE is deceptive because it's a performer too."

1977 Dodge Charger SE

1975 Dodge Charger SE

1975: "An all-new expression of personal luxury."

1976 Dodge Charger SE

1975 Dodge Charger SE standard interior

1977 Dodge Charger SE optional cloth & vinyl bucket seats

American Automotive Design Trends: The Personal Luxury Car

Dodge Magnum XE 1978-1979

1979 Dodge Magnum XE

1979 Dodge Magnum XE

1979 Dodge Magnum XE stand vinyl bucket seats (left) and optional leather bucket seats (right)

1978 Dodge Magnum XE

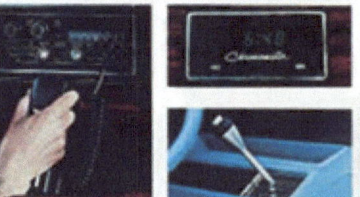 
1978 Dodge Magnum XE options

1979: "Rekindling the love affair between the car and the open road."

1979: "A tour-de-force of here-to-there excitement."

1979: "…the most luxurious Dodge for '79!"

Dodge Mirada 1980-1983

1981: "...Mirada is a unique collection of sensations."

1981 Dodge Mirada with CMX package

1981 Dodge Mirada with optional leather bucket seats

1982 Dodge Mirada

1982 Dodge Mirada

1982: "This is truly a modern and sporty personal-sized automobile."

1981 Dodge Mirada dash panel

1982: "An American road car that you'd never mistake for anything else."

1982 Dodge Mirada interior

American Automotive Design Trends: The Personal Luxury Car

Dodge Monaco 1965

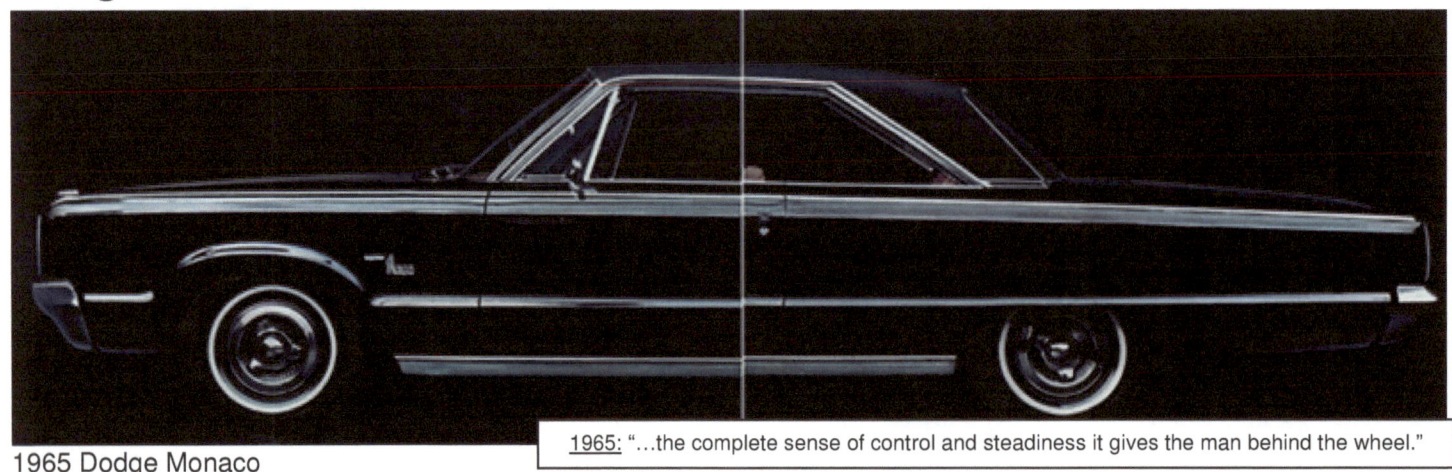

1965 Dodge Monaco

1965: "…the complete sense of control and steadiness it gives the man behind the wheel."

In 1966, Monaco becomes a full-line model.

1965: "You've never seen a Dodge like this before because there's never been a Dodge like this before. There is one model: the two-door hardtop."

1965: "It wears well with your sense of good taste."

1965 Dodge Monaco

1965 Dodge Monaco

American Automotive Design Trends: The Personal Luxury Car

Ford Elite 1974-1976

1976 Ford Elite

In 1974, the model is branded as the *Gran Torino Elite*. "Gran Torino" is dropped from the name in 1975.

1976 Ford Elite

1976 Ford Elite

1976 Ford Elite interiors

1976 Ford Elite

1975: "A mid-size car in the Thunderbird tradition."

1975: "It's designed with the craftsmanship, solid engineering, personal luxury and classic styling that have long been the tradition of Thunderbird."

1976: "Styling to keep you out of the crowd…"

1976: "It gives you so many ways to express your own tastes and flair. You can make it extra elegant, youthful or whatever suits your liking and lifestyle."

American Automotive Design Trends: The Personal Luxury Car

Ford Thunderbird 1955-1957

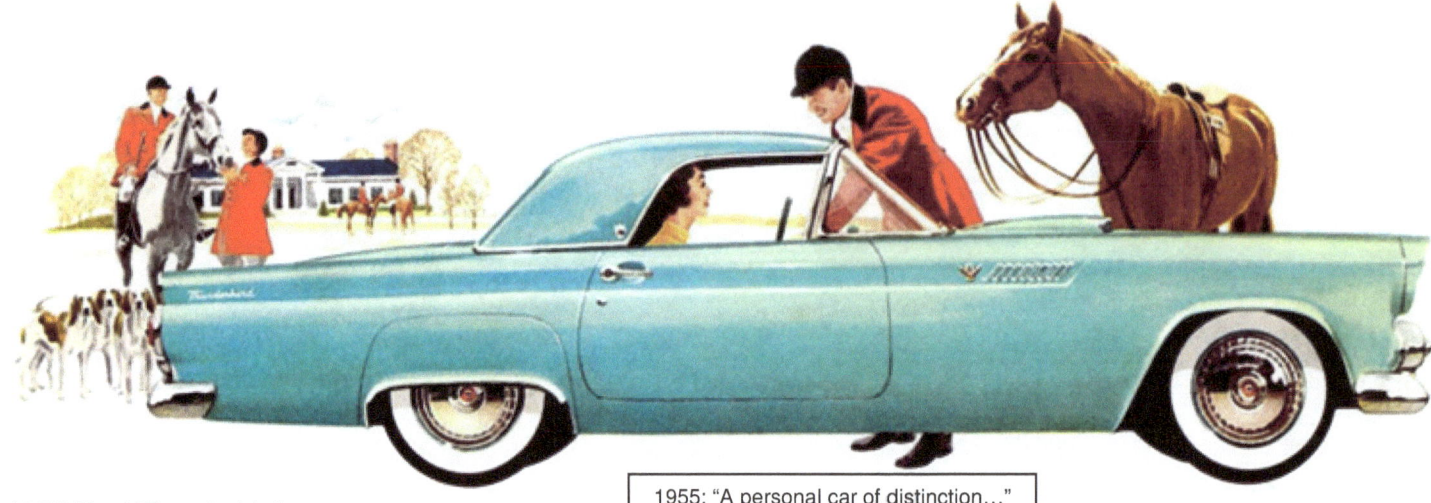

1955 Ford Thunderbird

1955: "A personal car of distinction…"

1956 Ford Thunderbird

1956: "It is for people such as you that this distinguished personal car was designed."

1955 Ford Thunderbird

1957 Ford Thunderbird

1957: "Strictly personal."

1957 Ford Thunderbird interior

1957: "Gentleman agree that the Thunderbird is America's distinguished personal car."

American Automotive Design Trends: The Personal Luxury Ca

Ford Thunderbird 1958-1960

1959 Ford Thunderbird

1958 Ford Thunderbird

1959 Ford Thunderbird

1959 Ford Thunderbird interior

1960 Ford Thunderbird

1958: "America's most individual car."

1959: "Thunderbird is young and sophisticated. Exciting and distinguished. Provocative and elegant."

1960: "Dashing as a sports car... Comfortable as a limousine."

1960 Ford Thunderbird

American Automotive Design Trends: The Personal Luxury Car

Ford Thunderbird 1961-1963

1962 Ford Thunderbird Landau

1961 Ford Thunderbird

1963 Ford Thunderbird

1961: "Thunderbird… unique in all the world."

1963: "Here are blended all the qualities that make an automobile a proud possession."

1961 Ford Thunderbird

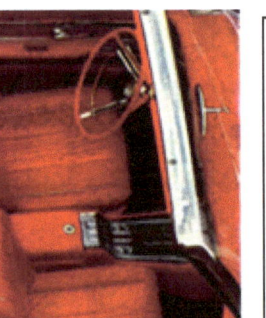
1961 Ford Thunderbird   1963 Ford Thunderbird

1963 Ford Thunderbird Sports Roadster

Ford Thunderbird 1964-1966

1964 Ford Thunderbird

1964 Ford Thunderbird

1964 Ford Thunderbird dash panel

1966 Ford Thunderbird Town Landau

1965: "The private world of Thunderbird…"

1965 Ford Thunderbird

1966 Ford Thunderbird

American Automotive Design Trends: The Personal Luxury Car

Ford Thunderbird 1972-1976

1975: "You can have it all your own way."

1976 Ford Thunderbird with Creme and Gold Luxury Group

1972 Ford Thunderbird

1972 Ford Thunderbird

1973 Ford Thunderbird   1974 Ford Thunderbird

1973: "For people going places who know how to go places."

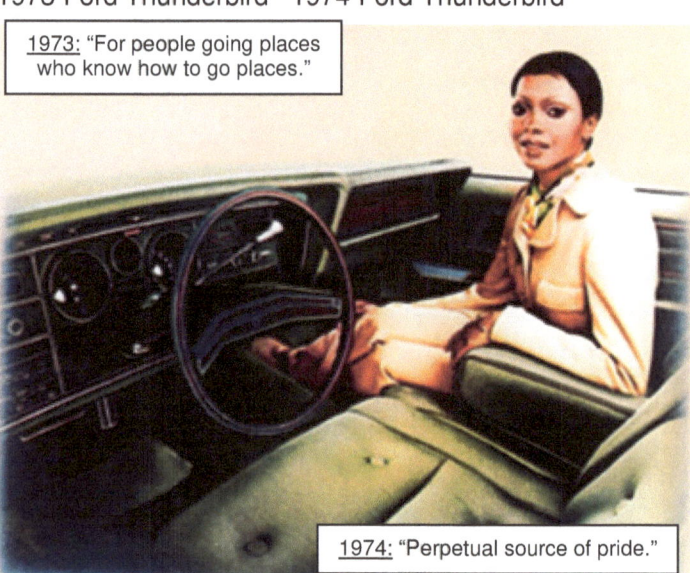

1974: "Perpetual source of pride."

1974 Ford Thunderbird dash panel and interior

46   American Automotive Design Trends: The Personal Luxury Ca

Ford Thunderbird 1977-1979

1977 Ford Thunderbird Town Landau

1977:
"No limit to luxury."
"Elegance begins here."
"Magnificent appointments."
"Styling alone makes it stand out from other personal luxury cars."

1979 Ford Thunderbird

1978 Ford Thunderbird with Sports Décor option

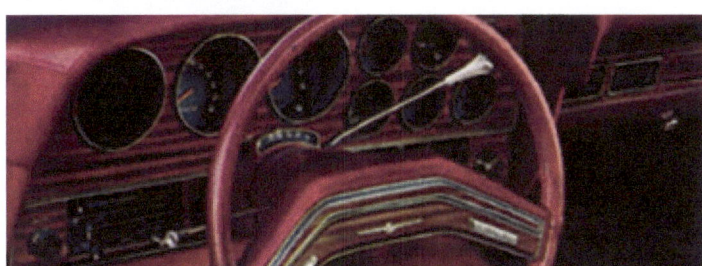
1979 Ford Thunderbird Heritage dash panel

1979 Ford Thunderbird with Sports Décor option

1977 Ford Thunderbird interior choices

American Automotive Design Trends: The Personal Luxury Car

Ford Thunderbird 1980-1982

1980 Ford Thunderbird Town Landau

1982: "...balances luxury with function."

1980 Ford Thunderbird dash panel with optional digital instrumentation

1982 Ford Thunderbird Heritage

1982 Ford Thunderbird Heritage

1980 Ford Thunderbird interior choices

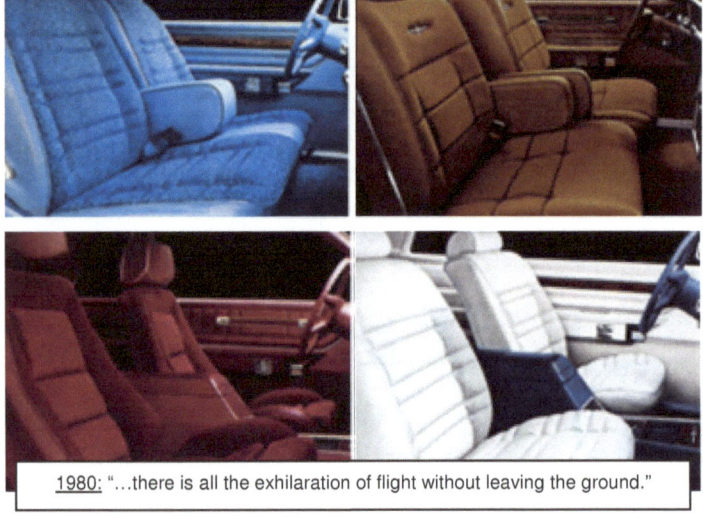

1980: "...there is all the exhilaration of flight without leaving the ground."

Ford Thunderbird 1983-1986

1983 Ford Thunderbird élan

1983: "Today's driver demands a car that responds eagerly to speed, steering and braking commands as if it were part of the driver... an extension of the five senses."

1984 Ford Thunderbird Turbo Coupe

1986 Ford Thunderbird

American Automotive Design Trends: The Personal Luxury Car 49

Ford Thunderbird 1987-1988

1987 Ford Thunderbird LX interior

1987: "…puts the emphasis on driving comfort."

1987 Ford Thunderbird optional digital instrumentation

1988 Ford Thunderbird LX

1987 Ford Thunderbird Turbo Coupe

1988 Ford Thunderbird

1988: "Thunderbird is a pleasure when it comes to your driving enjoyment."

Ford Thunderbird 1989-1997

1993 Ford Thunderbird

1993 Ford Thunderbird Super Coupe

1997 Ford Thunderbird

1989 Ford Thunderbird and interior

1993 Ford Thunderbird

> 1989: "...takes the art and science of design one step further with smooth clean lines that characterize the Ford approach to styling."
> 1993: "...synonymous with excellence in personal luxury and performance."

American Automotive Design Trends: The Personal Luxury Car   51

Ford Thunderbird 2002-2005

2005: "Spirited beauty."

2005 Ford Thunderbird 30th Anniversary Edition

2005 Ford Thunderbird

2005 Ford Thunderbird

2005 Ford Thunderbird

2002 Ford Thunderbird

Imperial 1981-1983

1982: "You have arrived."

1982 Imperial FS (Frank Sinatra edition)

1982 Imperial FS dash panel

1982 Imperial FS cloth interior

1982 Imperial

1982 Imperial

1983: "From every angle, Imperial makes a memorable statement about car and driver."

American Automotive Design Trends: The Personal Luxury Car

Lincoln Continental 1982-1987

1982: "In Continental, the classic and the contemporary are harmonized in one superbly styled automobile."

1982 Lincoln Continental Givenchy

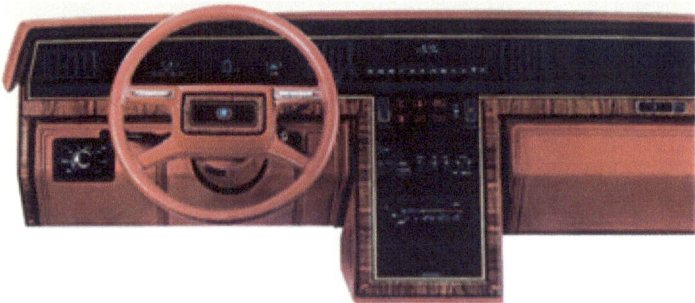

1982 Lincoln Continental dash panel

1985: "The personal sedan with alluring comfort."

1983 Lincoln Continental Givenchy

1984 Lincoln Continental Valentino

1987: "The first thing that you'll notice is that everybody else does."

1984 Lincoln Continental

1987 Lincoln Continental

American Automotive Design Trends: The Personal Luxury Ca

Lincoln Continental 1988-1994

1988 Lincoln Continental

1988 Lincoln Continental interior

1988 Lincoln Continental dash panel

1994 Lincoln Continental

1994 Lincoln Continental

> 1988: "...both the seen and the unseen make a difference."
>
> 1994: "An important part of Continental's special luxury is sophisticated engineering that brings added pleasure to drivers and exceptional comfort to anyone who goes along for the ride."
>
> 1994: "...boldly embodies what a luxury car should be."

American Automotive Design Trends: The Personal Luxury Car

Lincoln Continental 1995-2002

1995 Lincoln Continental

1997 Lincoln Continental interior

1998 Lincoln Continental dash panel

1998 Lincoln Continental

Lincoln Continental Mark III 1969-1971

1969: "The most authoritatively styled, decisively individual motorcar of this generation."

1969 Lincoln Continental Mark III

1969 Lincoln Continental Mark III rear seat

1971: "People want this car because it is something better."

1970 Lincoln Continental Mark III

1969 Lincoln Continental Mark III dash panel

1970 Lincoln Continental Mark III front seat

American Automotive Design Trends: The Personal Luxury Car

Lincoln Continental Mark IV 1972-1976

1973 Lincoln Continental Mark IV

1973   1974   1976

1972 Lincoln Continental Mark IV

1976 Lincoln Continental Mark IV

1973 Lincoln Continental Mark IV dash panel

1973: "This is the unique personal luxury car."

1976: "The Mark IV Designer Series could be the most dramatic concept of the personal luxury car in years."

1976 Lincoln Continental Mark IV designer series

Lincoln Continental Mark V 1977-1979

1977: "...everything a great luxury car should be."

1977 Lincoln Continental Mark V

1977 Lincoln Continental Mark V Bill Blass

1977 Lincoln Continental Mark V

1979: "Perhaps it's something you owe yourself."

1977 Lincoln Continental Mark V Bill Blass interior

1977 Lincoln Continental Mark V dash panel

American Automotive Design Trends: The Personal Luxury Car

Lincoln Continental Mark VII 1984-1992

1986: "...enhances the pure joy of driving."

1986 Lincoln Continental Mark VII LSC

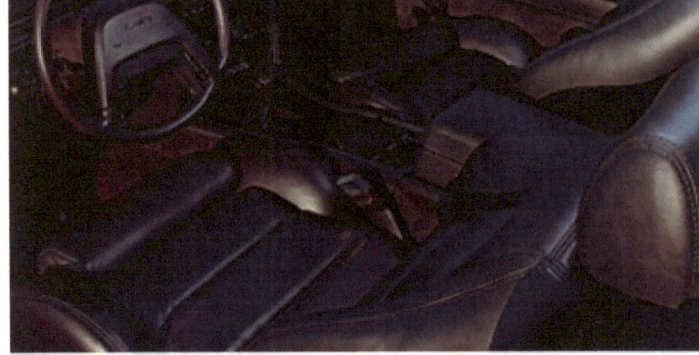

1986 Lincoln Continental Mark VII LSC interior

1986 Lincoln Continental Mark VII

1986: "Is it one of the best performing touring coupes in the world, or is it one of the most luxurious touring coupes in the world?"

American Automotive Design Trends: The Personal Luxury Car

Lincoln Continental Mark VIII 1993-1998

1998 Lincoln Continental Mark VIII

1998 Lincoln Continental Mark VIII

1993 Lincoln Continental Mark VIII interior and dash panel

1993 Lincoln Continental Mark VIII

1998: "We believe you'll agree that Mark VIII is precisely what a luxury car should be."

American Automotive Design Trends: The Personal Luxury Car

Lincoln Versailles 1977-1980

1980: "...enter a very special world created to gratify the most discriminating taste."

1980 Lincoln Versailles

1977 Lincoln Versailles

1977 Lincoln Versailles

1980 split bench interior

1977 flight bench interior

1977: "...created for those individuals who demand that their automobile reflect their own personal tastes and desires."

1977 Lincoln Versailles bucket seat and console option

1979 Lincoln Versailles dash panel

Mercury Cougar XR-7 1974-1976

1976 Mercury Cougar XR-7

1974 Mercury Cougar XR-7

1967 Mercury Cougar XR-7
(from "Luxury Sports Car" in 1967 to "Personal Luxury Car" in 1974)

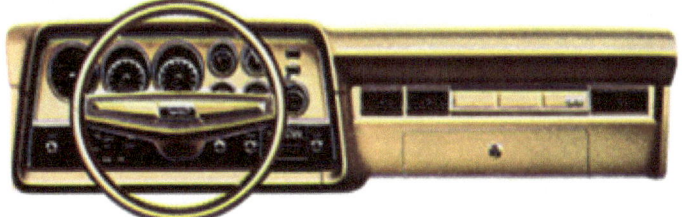
1974 Mercury Cougar XR-7 dash panel

1974 Mercury Cougar XR-7 split bench interior

1974 Mercury Cougar XR-7 bucket seat interior

1976: "…the luxurious personal-sized car that puts you way out in front of the rest!"

1976: "…sleek and sophisticated with its own personality."

American Automotive Design Trends: The Personal Luxury Car

Mercury Cougar XR-7 1977-1979

1977 Mercury Cougar XR-7

1977: "There's never been a Cougar so deeply elegant or styled with more sophisticated flair."

1977 Mercury Cougar XR-7 sports instrumentation

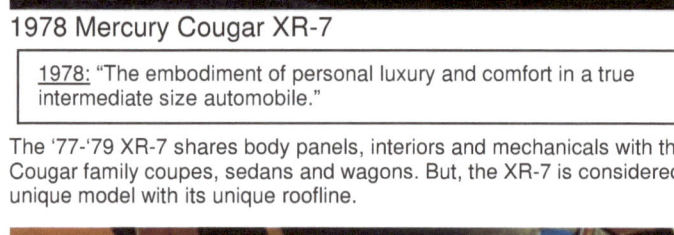

1978 Mercury Cougar XR-7

1978: "The embodiment of personal luxury and comfort in a true intermediate size automobile."

The '77-'79 XR-7 shares body panels, interiors and mechanicals with the Cougar family coupes, sedans and wagons. But, the XR-7 is considered a unique model with its unique roofline.

1977 Mercury Cougar XR-7 split bench interior

1978 Mercury Cougar XR-7 Midnight/Chamois décor option

American Automotive Design Trends: The Personal Luxury Car

Mercury Cougar XR-7 1980-1982

1980: "From a pedigree of personal luxury."

1980 Mercury Cougar XR-7 with Luxury Group

1980 Mercury Cougar XR-7 with Sports Group

1982: "A car made not for those who simply know where they're going, but for those who know exactly how to get there."

1982 Mercury Cougar XR-7 GS

1980 Mercury Cougar XR-7 optional digital instruments

1980 XR-7 Décor Group   1980 XR-7 Luxury Group

1980 Mercury Cougar XR-7 Sport Group with Recaro seats

1982 Mercury Cougar XR-7

American Automotive Design Trends: The Personal Luxury Car

Mercury Cougar 1983-1986

1983 Mercury Cougar LS interior

1983: "The future combines technology and craftsmanship for a new expression of personal luxury."

1983 Mercury Cougar

1985 optional digital gauges   1985 XR-7 gauges

1985: "...designed to put the driver's convenience, hence the driver's comfort, as the top priority."

1985: "The very fact that you arrive in a Cougar says that you've arrived."

1985 Mercury Cougar XR-7

1983 Mercury Cougar

1985 Mercury Cougar interior

In 1983, Mercury drops the "XR-7" badge from the Cougar name and "XR-7" becomes a performance and trim series of the Cougar.

66   American Automotive Design Trends: The Personal Luxury Ca

Mercury Cougar 1987-1988

1987 Mercury Cougar

1987 Mercury Cougar

1987: "A place where the driver is supremely comfortable while being very much in control."

1987: "One measure of a driver's car is how well it communicates with the driver."

1987 Mercury Cougar

1988 Mercury Cougar

American Automotive Design Trends: The Personal Luxury Car

Mercury Cougar 1989-1997

1989 Mercury Cougar

1989 Mercury Cougar XR-7 dash panel

> 1989: "Luxury, style and a unique level of comfort."

1989 Mercury Cougar

1991 Mercury Cougar XR-7

1997 Mercury Cougar

American Automotive Design Trends: The Personal Luxury Car

Mercury Marauder 1969-1970

1969 Mercury Marauder

1969 Mercury Marauder X-100

1970 Mercury Marauder

1969 Mercury Marauder X-100 interior

1970 Mercury Marauder X-100

1969: "Sports car action with a luxury look."

1969: "…makes a sporting thing of luxury."

1969: "…the elegant way to go all out."

1970 Mercury Marauder interior

American Automotive Design Trends: The Personal Luxury Car

Oldsmobile Aurora 1995-1999

1997 Oldsmobile Aurora

1997 Oldsmobile Aurora

Oldsmobile Aurora 2001-2003

2001 Oldsmobile Aurora

2001 Oldsmobile Aurora dash panel

<u>1997:</u> "Expressive, sensuous, assertive."

<u>1997:</u> "… a cockpit-inspired command center to stir your soul."

<u>2001:</u> "It's a meticulously crafted luxury performance sedan with the strength and balance to blaze a path far ahead of its pursuers, yet it displays a polished style that stands out from the crowd without disturbing it."

1997 Oldsmobile Aurora interior

2002 Oldsmobile Aurora interior

70   American Automotive Design Trends: The Personal Luxury Car

Oldsmobile Cutlass Supreme 1988-1989

1989: "This is not your father's Oldsmobile."

1989 Oldsmobile Cutlass Supreme International Series

Oldsmobile introduces a four-door sedan, in addition to the coupe, in 1990.

American Automotive Design Trends: The Personal Luxury Car

Oldsmobile Starfire 1961-1966

1961: "…with custom-built looks, luxury and power!"

1961 Oldsmobile Starfire — In 1961, Starfire was a trim series, not model, in convertible body only. Starfire becomes a unique model in 1962.

1962 Oldsmobile Starfire

1962: "Makes you master of all you survey."

1962 Oldsmobile Starfire convertible

1962 Oldsmobile Starfire interior

1964 Oldsmobile Starfire

1965 Oldsmobile Starfire

1965: "The car that makes luxury a sporting proposition!"

1965 Oldsmobile Starfire interior

72   American Automotive Design Trends: The Personal Luxury Car

Oldsmobile Toronado 1966-1970

1966: "An extraordinary kind of car for an extraordinary kind of person."

1966 Oldsmobile Toronado

1966 Oldsmobile Toronado

1968: "…unimpeachable one-of-a-kindness."

1966 Oldsmobile Toronado dash panel

1968 Oldsmobile Toronado

1970: "The ultimate escape machine."

1968 Oldsmobile Toronado interior   1970 Oldsmobile Toronado

American Automotive Design Trends: The Personal Luxury Car

Oldsmobile Toronado 1971-1978

1971: "The unmistakable one."

1971 Oldsmobile Toronado

1971 Oldsmobile Toronado

1975: "You've earned your rewards and deserve them."

1975 Oldsmobile Toronado

1977 Oldsmobile Toronado dash panel

1977: "A true classic - for those who cannot be content with the ordinary."

1972 Oldsmobile Toronado dash panel and interior

1977 Oldsmobile Toronado XSR

American Automotive Design Trends: The Personal Luxury Car

Oldsmobile Toronado 1979-1985

1981 Oldsmobile Toronado XSC

1979 Oldsmobile Toronado

1979: "A new state of the art in personal luxury car design."

1979 Oldsmobile Toronado interior

1980 Oldsmobile Toronado dash panel

1984 Oldsmobile Toronado

1984 Oldsmobile Toronado interior

1984: "A car this unique will probably become a prized addition for the serious collector."

1984 Oldsmobile Toronado Caliente

American Automotive Design Trends: The Personal Luxury Car

Oldsmobile Toronado 1986-1992

1986 Oldsmobile Toronado

1986 Oldsmobile Toronado dash panel and interior

1987 Oldsmobile Toronado Trofeo

1990 Oldsmobile Toronado Trofeo

Like its Buick Riviera stable mate, disappointing sales of the downsized 1986 models resulted in a refresh of the platform that increased the overall length of the car in 1989.

1990 Oldsmobile Toronado Trofeo

> 1986: "This is the shape of luxury performance."
>
> 1986: "The luxury of a complete electronic car."

Pontiac Grand Prix 1962-1968

1962: "The personally styled car with the power personality."

1962 Pontiac Grand Prix

1963   1964   1965

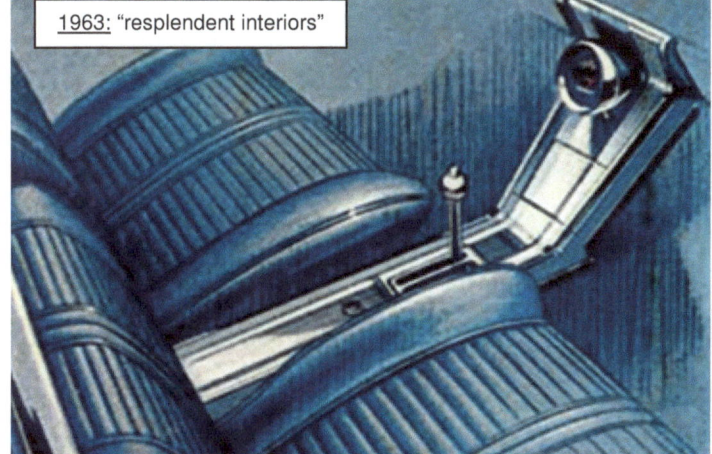

1963: "resplendent interiors"

1963 Pontiac Grand Prix interior

1968 Pontiac Grand Prix

1968: "Grand Prix has chaired the standards of personal luxury cars since its introduction."

1966 Pontiac Grand Prix

1966 Pontiac Grand Prix dash panel

1966: "So beautiful, in fact, its clean, aristocratic lines have set the standard for personal luxury cars."

1967 Pontiac Grand Prix

1967: "Who said you can't have everything?"

American Automotive Design Trends: The Personal Luxury Car

Pontiac Grand Prix 1969-1972

1969: "This machine was designed for one purpose - driving. Personal, luxurious, spirited driving."

1969 Pontiac Grand Prix SJ

1970 Pontiac Grand Prix

1970: "We don't build a "luxury" car. We build a performance car, then make it luxurious. Beauty without frills. Comfort without boredom. Luxury with spirit."

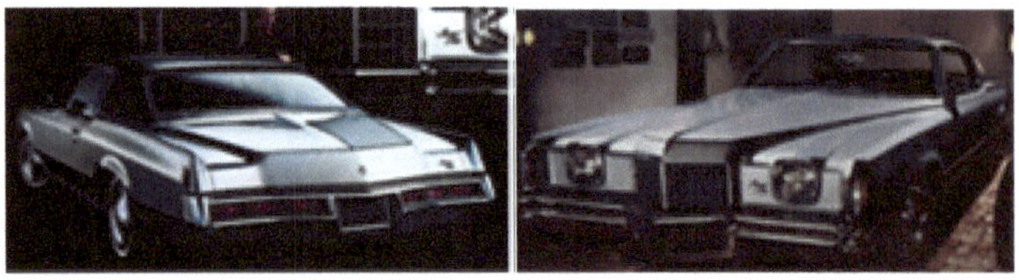

1972 Pontiac Grand Prix

1972: "…styling is as distinctive to Grand Prix as your fingerprints are to you."

1970 Pontiac Grand Prix interior

Pontiac Grand Prix 1973-1977

1973 Pontiac Grand Prix

1974 Pontiac Grand Prix

1974 Pontiac Grand Prix

1976 Pontiac Grand Prix

1976 Pontiac Grand Prix dash panel

1976 Pontiac Grand Prix bucket seat interior

1976 Pontiac Grand Prix flight bench interior

1976: "Pontiac's classic personal car."

American Automotive Design Trends: The Personal Luxury Car

Pontiac Grand Prix 1978-1980

1978 Pontiac Grand Prix SJ

1978: "This year, a dramatically new car has earned the right to bear the Grand Prix name. To symbolize Pontiac's dedication to styling flair and performance. To engineering innovation and luxury that never gets in the way of driving."

1980 Pontiac Grand Prix LJ

1980 Pontiac Grand Prix LJ interior

1979 Pontiac Grand Prix bucket seat interior

American Automotive Design Trends: The Personal Luxury Car

Pontiac Grand Prix 1981-1987

1981 Pontiac Grand Prix LJ

1984 Pontiac Grand Prix LJ

1981 Pontiac Grand Prix bucket seat interior

1981 Pontiac Grand Prix LJ interior

1986 Pontiac Grand Prix

1986 Pontiac Grand Prix

American Automotive Design Trends: The Personal Luxury Car

Pontiac Grand Prix 1988-1989

1989 Pontiac Grand Prix LE

In 1990, like the Regal and Cutlass, Pontiac adds a four-door model to the Grand Prix nameplate.

1989 Pontiac Grand Prix digital instrumentation

1989: "A blend of humanity and machine."

1989: "Apart from its come-hither appearance, there's a lot of beauty in the details of Grand Prix."

1989 Pontiac Grand Prix interior

1988 Pontiac Grand Prix LE

1988 Pontiac Grand Prix SE

Studebaker Avanti 1963-1964

1963: "The Avanti is a car with a unique dual personality… that of an elegant prestige car and a car of high performance."

1963 Studebaker Avanti
Avanti continues to be sold after 1964 by a two dealers that purchased the tooling and model name after Studebaker closed the factory.

1963: "Action car… for luxury lovers."

1963 Studebaker Avanti

1963 Studebaker Avanti interiors

1964 Studebaker Avanti

1964: "But mere speed potential is unimportant compared with Avanti's elegant way of making the most routine trip a thrilling experience."

American Automotive Design Trends: The Personal Luxury Car

Studebaker Hawk 1956-1961

1961 Studebaker Hawk

1957 Studebaker Golden Hawk

1957 Studebaker Silver Hawk

1957 Studebaker Golden Hawk interior

1957 Studebaker Golden Hawk dash panel

1957: "Adventure begins with the turn of a key."
1957: "This is a car that restores the fun and excitement to luxury motoring."

Studebaker Gran Turismo Hawk 1962-1964

1962 Studebaker Gran Turismo Hawk

1962: "… the luxurious embodiment of roadability and driving ease… a boldly dramatic automobile designed in the meticulous tradition of the great European road cars."

1962 Studebaker Gran Turismo Hawk

1963 Studebaker Gran Turismo Hawk

1963: "Classic styling… timeless elegance…"

1963 Studebaker Gran Turismo Hawk interior

1963: "…truly an automobile for connoisseurs!"

1962 Studebaker Gran Turismo Hawk dash panel & interior

1964 Studebaker Gran Turismo Hawk

American Automotive Design Trends: The Personal Luxury Car

Specifications

Generation		Make	Model	Engine Displacements in Liters	Wheelbase in Inches
Start	Last				
1988	1991	Buick	Reatta	3.8V6	98.5
1978	1980	Buick	Regal	3.2V6, 3.8V6, 3.8V6 Turbo	108
1981	1981	Buick	Regal	3.8V6, 3.8V6 Turbo	108
1985	1987	Buick	Regal	3.8V6, 3.8V6 Turbo, 4.3V6 Diesel, 5.0V8	108
1988	1989	Buick	Regal	2.8V6, 3.1V6	107.5
1963	1965	Buick	Riviera	6.6V8, 7.0V8	117
1966	1970	Buick	Riviera	7.0V8, 7.5V8	119
1971	1973	Buick	Riviera	7.5V8	122
1974	1976	Buick	Riviera	7.5V8	122
1977	1978	Buick	Riviera	5.7V8, 6.6V8	115.9
1979	1985	Buick	Riviera	3.8V6, 3.8V6 Turbo, 4.1V6, 5.0V8, 5.7V8, 5.7V8 Diesel	114
1986	1993	Buick	Riviera	3.8V6	108
1995	1999	Buick	Riviera	3.8V6, 3.8V6 Supercharged	113.8
1987	1993	Cadillac	Allante	4.1V8, 4.5V8, 4.6V8	99.4
1967	1970	Cadillac	Eldorado	7.0V8, 7.7V8, 8.2V8	120
1971	1978	Cadillac	Eldorado	7.0V8, 8.2V8	126.3
1979	1985	Cadillac	Eldorado	4.1V6, 4.1V8, 5.7V8, 5.7V8 Diesel, 6.0V8	114
1986	1991	Cadillac	Eldorado	4.1V8, 4.9V8	108
1992	2002	Cadillac	Eldorado	4.6V8, 4.9V8	108
1975	1979	Cadillac	Seville	5.7V8	114.3
1980	1985	Cadillac	Seville	4.1V8, 5.7V8, 5.7V8 Diesel, 6.0V8	114
1986	1991	Cadillac	Seville	4.1V8	108
1992	1997	Cadillac	Seville	4.6V8, 4.9V8	111
1998	2004	Cadillac	Seville	4.6V8	112.2
1970	1972	Chevrolet	Monte Carlo	5.7V8, 6.5V8, 7.4V8	116
1973	1977	Chevrolet	Monte Carlo	5.0V8, 5.7V8, 6.5V8, 7.4V8	116
1978	1980	Chevrolet	Monte Carlo	3.3V6, 3.8V6, 3.8V6 Turbo, 4.4V8, 5.0V8	108
1981	1988	Chevrolet	Monte Carlo	3.8V6, 3.8V6 Turbo, 4.3V8, 5.0V8, 5.7V8	108
1995	1999	Chevrolet	Monte Carlo	3.1V6, 3.4V6, 3.8V6	107.5
2000	2007	Chevrolet	Monte Carlo	3.4V6, 3.5V6, 3.8V6, 3.9V6, 5.3V8	110.5
1955	1956	Chrysler	300	5.4V8	126
1957	1959	Chrysler	300	5.8V8, 6.4V8, 6.8V8	126
1960	1961	Chrysler	300	6.8V8	126
1975	1979	Chrysler	Cordoba	5.2V8, 5.9V8, 6.6V8	115
1980	1983	Chrysler	Cordoba	3.7L6, 5.2V8	112.7
1989	1991	Chrysler	TC Maserati	2.2L4, 3.0V6	93.3
1956	1957	Continental	Mark II	6.0V8	126
1975	1978	Dodge	Charger SE	5.2V8, 5.9V8, 6.6V8	115
1978	1979	Dodge	Magnum	5.2V8, 5.9V8, 6.6V8	115
1980	1983	Dodge	Mirada	3.7L6, 5.2V8	112.7
1965	1965	Dodge	Monaco	6.3V8	121
1974	1976	Ford	Elite	5.8V8, 6.6V8, 7.5V8	114
1955	1957	Ford	Thunderbird	4.8V8, 5.1V8	102
1958	1960	Ford	Thunderbird	5.8V8, 7.0V8	113
1961	1963	Ford	Thunderbird	6.4V8	113

Specifications

Generation					Wheelbase
Start	Last	Make	Model	Engine Displacements in Liters	in Inches
1964	1966	Ford	Thunderbird	6.4V8, 7.0V8	113.2
1972	1976	Ford	Thunderbird	7.5V8	120.4
1977	1979	Ford	Thunderbird	5.0V8, 5.8V8, 6.6V8	114
1980	1982	Ford	Thunderbird	3.3V6, 3.8V6, 4.2V8, 5.0V8	108.4
1983	1986	Ford	Thunderbird	2.3L4 Turbo, 3.8V6, 5.0V8	104.2
1987	1988	Ford	Thunderbird	2.3L4 Turbo, 3.8V6, 5.0V8	104.2
1989	1997	Ford	Thunderbird	3.8V6, 3.8V6 Supercharged, 4.6V8, 5.0V8	113
2002	2005	Ford	Thunderbird	3.9V8	107.2
1981	1983	Imperial	Imperial	5.2V8	112.7
1982	1987	Lincoln	Continental	2.4L6 Diesel, 5.0V8	108.5
1988	1994	Lincoln	Continental	3.8V6	109
1995	1997	Lincoln	Continental	4.6V8	109
1998	2002	Lincoln	Continental	4.6V8	109
1968	1971	Lincoln	Mark III	7.5V8	117.2
1972	1976	Lincoln	Mark IV	7.5V8	120.4
1977	1979	Lincoln	Mark V	6.6V8, 7.5V8	120.4
1984	1992	Lincoln	Mark VII	2.4L6 Diesel, 5.0V8	108.5
1993	1998	Lincoln	Mark VIII	4.6V8	113
1977	1980	Lincoln	Versailles	5.0V8, 5.8V8	109.9
1974	1976	Mercury	Cougar XR-7	5.8V8, 6.6V8, 7.5V8	114
1977	1979	Mercury	Cougar XR-7	5.0V8, 5.8V8, 6.6V8	114
1980	1982	Mercury	Cougar XR-7	3.8V6, 4.2V8, 5.0V8	108.4
1983	1986	Mercury	Cougar	2.3L4 Turbo, 3.8V6, 5.0V8	104
1987	1988	Mercury	Cougar	2.3L4 Turbo, 3.8V6, 5.0V8	104
1989	1997	Mercury	Cougar	3.8V6, 4.6V8, 5.0V8	113
1969	1970	Mercury	Marauder	6.4V8, 7.0V8	121
1995	1999	Oldsmobile	Aurora	4.0V8	113.8
2001	2003	Oldsmobile	Aurora	3.5V6, 4.0V8	112.2
1988	1989	Oldsmobile	Cutlass Supreme	2.8V6, 3.1V6	107.5
1962	1966	Oldsmobile	Starfire	6.5V8, 7.0V8	123
1966	1970	Oldsmobile	Toronado	7.0V8, 7.5V8	119
1971	1978	Oldsmobile	Toronado	6.6V8, 7.5V8	122
1979	1985	Oldsmobile	Toronado	4.1V6, 5.0V8, 5.7V8, 5.7V8 Diesel	114
1986	1992	Oldsmobile	Toronado	3.8V6	108
1962	1968	Pontiac	Grand Prix	6.4V8, 6.6V8, 6.9V8, 7.0V8	120 & 121
1969	1972	Pontiac	Grand Prix	6.6V8, 7.0V8, 7.4V8	118
1973	1977	Pontiac	Grand Prix	5.0V8, 6.6V8, 7.0V8, 7.4V8	116
1978	1980	Pontiac	Grand Prix	3.8V6, 4.3V8, 5.0V8	108
1981	1987	Pontiac	Grand Prix	3.8V6, 4.1V6, 5.0V8, 5.7V8 Diesel	108
1988	1989	Pontiac	Grand Prix	2.8V6, 3.1V6	107.5
1963	1964	Studebaker	Avanti	4.7V8	109
1956	1961	Studebaker	Hawk	2.8V6, 4.2V8, 4.7V8	121
1962	1964	Studebaker	GT Hawk	4.7V8, 5.0V8 Supercharged	121

Honorable Mention

Because most of the Silver Star cars in this book were based on mainstream family sedans, sharing mechanicals and many décor pieces, it would not be a stretch to label some of those family cars as a Personal Luxury Car. Often, these cars were recognized as Personal Luxury Car candidates by their trim level designations, such as Brougham, Limited, Ghia, Special Edition and more. Yet, because they shared their model name and body panels with these full model lines of coupes, sedans and wagon, they at best deserve an Honorable Mention for Personal Luxury Car status.

Of particular interest are the GM Colonnade models of the 1970s. While Chevrolet and Pontiac had the unique models of Monte Carlo and Grand Prix, respectively, these cars were based on the Malibu and Lemans. The Monte Carlo's and Grand Prix's interiors and engine choices were similar to the family cars while the sheet metal and names were unique. When compared to the offerings from Buick's and Oldsmobile's Colonnade models, these makes' lacked a unique body and name, though the Century/Cutlass lines could be lavishly outfitted. However, without the distinctive body and name, the appeal of personal luxury is weakened.

Additional, examples of automobiles that may be trim series of existing models include the AMC Matador Barcelona, Buick Invicta Wildcat, Chrysler LeBaron, Ford Torino, Mercury Montego, Plymouth Fury, the Studebaker Champion / Commander / President and more. Because size matters, these intermediate length automobiles still cast their presence while remaining intimate which is part of the Personal Luxury Car quality.

A case could even be made that subcompact and compact size cars with higher trim levels could approach the status of Personal Luxury Car. Automobiles such as the AMC Concord D/L, Ford Granada / Mercury Monarch Ghia, Dodge Aspen / Plymouth Volare Special Edition, Chevrolet Nova Concours, Ford Mustang II Ghia and more could be well appointed. However, the smaller size, same body panels and mass production relegates them to family car grading.

AMC Matador Barcelona

1978 AMC Matador Brougham Barcelona

While sharing the four-door's Matador name, AMC did manage to give the coupe unique sheet metal. Adding the Barcelona badge and trim (on top of the required Brougham level) propelled it to near luxury status. AMC called it "a mid-size value with outstanding appeal."

Buick Invicta Wildcat

1962 Buick Invicta Wildcat

In 1962, the Wildcat was a trim series of the Buick Invicta, available as a coupe and convertible. The Wildcat uses Electra like taillights and added a bucket seat interior. Buick, then, in 1963 expanded the Wildcat to a separate model line and added four-door hardtop and sedan models.

Buick Regal

1973 Buick Century Regal

Unlike Chevrolet's Monte Carlo, the Regal was a trim series of the Century model line in 1973. From 1974 through 1977, Regal became a separate full line model of two- and four-door cars. In 1978, Regal would become a unique two-door model only. Yet, Buick would play the shell game with names and in 1982, the former Century sedan is called Regal while the Century name is applied to a new front-wheel-drive family sedan.

Chrysler LeBaron

1978 Chrysler LeBaron

1988 Chrysler LeBaron

The LeBaron became a best-selling model for Chrysler. Like the Oldsmobile Cutlass, the name was applied to many designs including two-doors, four-doors, wagons (Town and Country), convertibles and hatchbacks (1985-1989 GTS). The model line started in 1977 and the name was shelved in 1995. From 1987 to 1995, the Chrysler LeBaron coupe and convertible had a unique body and interior, but shared its name with the sedans.

Dodge 400 / 600

1983 Dodge 400

The sister car of the Chrysler LeBaron, Dodge introduced the 400 in 1982 when the LeBaron was downsized to the K-car front-wheel-drive platform. The car came as a coupe, convertible and sedan. In 1984, Dodge renames the car as the 600 and later will replace the sedan with a larger wheelbase platform that underpinned the Plymouth Caravelle.

Dodge Diplomat

1978 Dodge Diplomat

Again, Dodge re-badges a Chrysler for its entry into the near luxury car field. Called the Diplomat, this model line includes a coupe, sedan and wagon. In 1982, the range is reduced to a four-door sedan with an emphasis on family car value and fleet sales as taxis and police cars.

Ford Thunderbird 1967-1971

1967 Ford Thunderbird

This entry into the Honorable Mentions category will no doubt raise a few eyebrows and objections. After all, it's a Thunderbird; the very car that perhaps defined Personal Luxury more than any other nameplate.

So why is it on this list? The answer is simple, if not debatable. By adding a four-door model, the model line becomes less personal and design for mass appeal with larger volume sales.

American Automotive Design Trends: The Personal Luxury Car

Ford Torino

1974 Ford Torino

Ford used the Torino name on their intermediate chassis from 1968 through 1976. It is with the 1972-1976 re-design that the Torino could be moved upscale with their optional appointments on a "Gran Torino" trim series.

In 1974, Ford introduces the Gran Torino Elite with smoother sheet metal on the quarter panel and unique opera windows. Ford drops the 'Gran Torino" moniker for 1975 and 1976 and simply calls the model Elite. (See page 41.)

In 1977 the Thunderbird was down-sized on an updated Torino platform. At this time, the Torino name was replaced with LTD II.

Lincoln Continental (1961-1965)

1961 Lincoln Continental

Based on the Thunderbird, Lincoln introduces the new Continental in 1961 and becomes an instant success and sensation. It is sold as a four-door model only in both sedan and convertible models. Compared to the contemporary luxury cars of the time, the new Lincoln is smaller and appears more intimate and understated. Yet, it appears on the list of Honorable Mentions because it is Lincoln's only entry in the full-size luxury car market intended for volume sales.

Lincoln Continental Mark VI

1981 Lincoln Continental Mark VI

The Mark VI is the only Mark in the series, started in 1968, not considered a Personal Luxury Car. Based on the Town Car and Town Coupe of the era, the Mark VI came in two-door and four-door models. They were better appointed than their Town Car brethren, but lacked the intimacy and reduced scale associated with personal luxury.

Mercury Montego

1974 Mercury Montego MX

The Mercury Montego shares a similar history with the Ford Torino. It could be appointed with Brougham styling that lifted its stature close to personal luxury. However, that status was given to the 1974 Mercury Cougar XR-7. In 1977, the Montego name would disappear and the re-styled model is badged Cougar without the XR-7 designation.

Oldsmobile Cutlass

1981 Oldsmobile Cutlass

The Cutlass is Oldsmobile biggest success story. It was so successful, that Oldsmobile would use the Cutlass name on many platforms and attach various names to it, such as Cutlass Salon, Cutlass Supreme, Cutlass Ciera and Cutlass Cruiser. This is great for mass market selling but dilutes the mystique of individuality that luxury car buyers expect. As platforms change in later years, the rear-wheel-drive Cutlass Supreme becomes a "Classic" as a two-door only model in 1988, for one year only. In that same year, Olds introduces a front-wheel-drive Cutlass Supreme, two-door coupe, without the "Classic" badge. By 1990, the Cutlass Supreme again will become a full model line.

Plymouth Fury

1975 Plymouth Fury

Like the Dodge Coronet, Plymouth fielded the Fury in 1975 as a mid-size family sedan that could be appointed to luxury car levels, with and without opera windows. However, unlike Dodge's Cordoba clones, Plymouth did not have a unique model to launch as a Personal Luxury Car.

Pontiac Bonneville (1984-1986)

1984 Pontiac Bonneville Brougham

Here too is another example of a model that experience several name changes and brand confusion. In the early 1980s, the Pontiac Bonneville was a full-size car. With the downsizing trends of the era, Pontiac drops the full-size car and applies the Bonneville badge to the former mid-size Lemans sedan and wagon. From 1984 to 1986, the Bonneville is sold as an entry luxury sedan only and in 1987 it becomes a full-size front-wheel drive family sedan.

Studebaker Champion, Commander and President

1954 Studebaker Commander Regal Starliner coupe

From 1953 through 1955, Studebaker sold coupe versions of their Champion, Commander and President models. Though they shared names and mechanicals, the body panels and wheelbase were unique to the coupes. In 1956, Studebaker began applying the Hawk brand to their coupes to distinguish them from the family sedans.

American Automotive Design Trends: The Personal Luxury Car

INDEX

3
300 .... 30, 31, 32

4
400 89

6
600 89

A
Allante 16
Aurora 70
Avanti 83

B
Bonneville 91

C
Champion 91
Charge SE 37
Commander 91
Continental 54, 55, 56, 90
Cordoba 2, 33, 34
Cougar 63, 64, 65, 66, 67, 68
Cutlass 91
Cutlass Supreme 71

D
Diplomat 89

E
Eldorado 17, 18, 19, 20
Elite 41

F
Fury 91

G
Gran Turismo Hawk 85
Grand Prix 77, 78, 79, 80, 81, 82

H
Hawk 84

I
Imperial 53
Invicta 88

L
LeBaron 89

M
Magnum XE 38
Marauder 69
Mark II 36
Mark III 57
Mark IV 58
Mark V 59
Mark VI 90
Mark VII 60
Mark VIII 61
Matador 88
Mirada 39
Monaco 40
Monte Carlo 25, 26, 27, 28, 29
Montego 90

P
President 91

R
Reatta 4
Regal 5, 6, 7, 88
Riviera 8, 9, 10, 11, 12, 13, 14, 15

S
Seville 21, 22, 23, 24
Starfire 72

T
TC by Maserati 35
Thunderbird 42, 43, 44, 45, 46, 47, 48, 49, 50, 51, 52, 89
Torino 90
Toronado 73, 74, 75, 76

V
Versailles 62

W
Wildcat 88

X
XR-7 .... 63, 64, 65, 66, 67, 68

www.ingramcontent.com/pod-product-compliance
Lightning Source LLC
Chambersburg PA
CBHW040906020526
44114CB00037B/72